This plane is going to crash

a collection of poems

Maurice Jovan Billington

This Plane is Going to Crash
Copyright © Maurice Jovan Billingham 2015
ISBN-13: 978-0991608829
ISBN-10: 0991608828

Cover and author images © Kris Misevski
Cover design © Greg Harvey
Interior design © DeAnna Knippling

Courtney Literary, LLC, Colorado Springs
www.courtneyliterary.com

this plane
is going
to crash

untitled

open window
autumn
breeze blows
regret
autumn leaves
caress
shattered pane
shirtless soul
refrain
wake up
make up
wrapped around your body

blue sky liar

blue pt. 1
he would remember the day
and say the sky was blue
but all she remembers is rain
no, i'd say
i remember the day
but all she remembers is rain
when i made you laugh
when i held your hand
when i saw you smile
when i was your man?
all she remembers is rain
he would remember the day
and say the sky was blue

blue pt. 2
look at it
with your eyes closed
the way i wanted you
to look at me
so you could not see
blue

(blue interlude)
and you will leave
blue

blue pt. 3
how many times do i have to say it before you believe me?

blue pt. 4
and will you be
and will you believe
blue
and will you be
and will you leave
blue

lit

cigarette in your hand
i puff
blow
smoke evaporates
but the touch of your finger
lingers

dead deer along the roadside

i'm sure it was smiling
once
it's sunday morning
hi god

dead deer along the roadside (version 2)

there's a dead deer along the roadside
if you do cocaine until 6am
it will come to you
and ask why you are still awake
before it leaves it will ask for a cookie
you should give it to him
but don't offer him milk
he can't drink that
he's dead

dead deer along the roadside (version 3)

who told you life was beautiful
it's nothing but heartache and pain
you are born into a Cure song
sing along
and don't complain
yeah
i saw you through my windshield
move motherfucker
move
why should i go around
i know you're beautiful
that's why we were fated to crash
because nothing beautiful last
and baby you're not that fast
to get out of my way
why are you even out here
why does no one stop for deer

dead deer along the roadside
(final version)

saw a dead deer along the roadside
almost made me cry
made me think of my son
innocence isn't maturity
until it's hit by a speeding car
sometimes you don't survive
makes you not want to drive
but you have to to live
but you have to to give
maybe god isn't that wise
maybe life isn't that nice
maybe i'm just drunk
but i don't want to think about that deer anymore

between the blue and the violet

rainbow falls
pitch bright
colors
without you
blue

black light
lit
violet
searching still
you

sadness bleeds
happiness pleased… to meet me
caught between the two shades of
you

rainbow falls
searching still
happiness
indigo
you

masada

this is my sacrifice
that i will let myself be destroyed by the pain of loving you
before i am destroyed by the thought of living without you

timbre-wolf

head over hills
in fields of paramours
sugar hiccups
sugar hiccups
he only wants more
than is ever allowed
garlands and gray zones
pale clouded and white
which belongs
which is wrong
right
he says i love you
only half joking
like some fifty-fifty clown
all that is allowed
pandora or Lorelei
iceblink twins
she sings like Liz
sugar hiccup
sunburst or snow-blind
everytime
her fingers across the keys
the timbre in her voice

the tremble in a choice
blind dumb deaf
heaven or Las Vegas
all that is left
things like Liz
can never be his

bete noir

you looked away from me
into my eyes
if you can understand why fire avoids rain
then you can understand
my pain
as your tear pierced my skin
when your face brushed mine
to say good-bye
now my neck burns
scarred where your mouth touched
leaving me breathless and dying
with a tortured thought of what might have been
had you not swayed
to avoid
the consequence
of my lips

this plane is going to crash

last cigarette
i know, i promised
but why would you believe me
people don't stop smoking
just like planes don't fly
how could they, they're too heavy, the air is too thin
and i need a cigarette
just to pretend
that this relationship is not going to end
have i made you upset
then you should curse god
he created physics
he broke your heart
he made you believe planes could fly
when it's obvious
they can't
how could they, they're too heavy, the air is too thin
and now it's getting harder to breath
by the way i like that dress
it will look pretty when you leave
no i'm not asking
and it won't matter if we fasten
our seatbelts

and it doesn't matter how we felt
on takeoff
and it doesn't matter if you take off
that dress
don't blame me for the mess
beneath
it's no longer so sweet
how you believe planes can fly
they can't, they're too heavy, the air is too thin
i think i see the horizon
coming fast
faster than it should
i wish you would
have listened to me
i told you that it would
now you're going to cry
it's alright
God fucked us with hearts and gravity the moment we were born

jordan

i saw a piece of paper
pain
don't cry when it rains
sorrow

when your eyes look at me what do i see
yours
his
mine
i can't find... words
so much to answer for
i don't know if it matters anymore
if it matters more
to you
or to
me

i saw a piece of paper
plain
where you had written down names
one of them was
Jordan

nails

nails she used to scratch lines in her arm
like trenches of sorrow she withdrew into

benediction

how much do you love me?
as much as when we kiss
and your eyelashes wave to forever
as your eyes shut…

that's when i believe
when i am caught between infinity
which is the crush of your eyes closing
and the kiss of your lips

I-IV

I: glimmer
why do your eyes shine when they look at me
don't you know i'll run and hide
don't you care
find me
save me
if you dare
pull me from this darkness and let me drown in your glimmer

II: submersion
let me drown in your glimmer
where
love will need me
love will bleed me
love… is
blind

III: slip
i love you…
blind

IV: petals
i am falling
a tear from the sky
unafraid
because i will land in your arms
safe
i am
protected…
by you
like the petals of the flower that catch the rain so that it never touches the ground

sometimes he said

sometimes it would rain
and then her flowers thrived
sometimes isn't always enough
and so she watched them die
sometimes he said i love you…
sometimes

beautiful wreck

i knew your lips were trouble
i should have taped them shut
you don't need them anyway
you talk with your eyes
fucking disaster
don't close them i'm not finished talking
i told you
but all you want to do is shut me up
by putting me in your mouth
i'm a mess
and you're no better
you know it it only makes you wetter
i'm a wreck
and you are beautiful…
i felt your legs were trouble
why didn't you walk away
was it because they were wrapped around me
and how many times have you found me
between them
between us
you taste like the day i forgot to wear my boots in the snow
cold then warm
makes me feel like a kid again

i miss that
you bliss that
and i will wipe that smile from your
face
like memories that melt
leaving no trace
i will still be beautiful
and you will be a wreck…
close your eyes now

sometimes he said pt. 2

sometimes he said things that were good
sometimes he said things that he should
always his words were carefully spent
only sometimes he said things that he meant

cartier

i look at her from the corner of my eye, that's all i'm allowed
lest someone know how i feel
eyes betray…
she taps a cigarette, cartier
tap, tap, tap
but the ashes won't fall
i laugh to myself because i know she can't love me
but i still call
though now i only watch
as the ashes finally fall, and her attention turns to the label
on a bottle of water that has touched
her lips… her lips… her lips…
tap, tap, tap…
she rips the label from the bottle, methodically etching a
line around the circumference
until it is torn,
torn between what is right
and unrequited
but that is me, the label just ripped-
now she is tired, so i watch as she rests her chin on the cap
of the bottle

and i wish it was my shoulder,
she knows she looks at me and smiles,
what she doesn't know is that i have already written what i would say
before the last ash has fallen from her cartier

debris

i witnessed a fire that was the consequence of love
but my eyes were too wet to burn
the sadness of decay, no the decay of sadness
that's what she was
as she blew a kiss to extinguish the flames
and i looked down at what remained
his ashes
scattered
like a butterfly torn apart by the wind

tremors

it had been so long since i held your hand
so long, so long
so long as you understand
that when i touched you
i felt a tremor
that went from my heart to my head
and sent me whirling out of control
like a hummingbird in flames
so i searched desperately for safety
and looked into your eyes
your eyes, your eyes
your eyes look so beautiful when reflected in the fire of my
insecurity
that i blushed
then rushed
to look away
mistake
for i glanced at your smile
then focused on your lips
but you have to understand
it was impossible to resist
and i felt a tremor
and almost died

carnal knowledge

don't look at me
because you know i want to fuck you
because you can see it in my eyes
when i look at you and say
i love you, when i want to say
i want to fuck you
because i love you
and this love is too strong to make love
when i haven't seen you for so long
so don't look at me
if you cannot handle forever
whether it's the look in my eye
or whatever
that says i want to fuck you
until our bodies bleed together

isosceles

i think the word is isosceles
having two equal sides
because i want you
as much as i need you
as much as i want you
it's almost a circle
not a triangle
the uneven line being my fear
shaped by my desire to overcome it
into a curve
i don't look at you like
he did
or he did
or he did
their want is obtuse
there is nothing
sharp or defined in the way they want to hold you
i want to hold you as you have held me
to be your equal line
you know
having two equal sides
i think the word is…
isosceles

the confusion of sighs
(when rendered with goodbye)

when you kissed me goodbye
were you kissing me goodbye
the look in your eye
was it saying goodbye
the press of your lips
did i imagine you sigh
the caress of your flesh
was i feeling you cry
when you kissed me goodbye did you kiss me goodbye
love dies love dies love dies
goodbye

7 seconds

i stared into your eyes for six seconds
and during the seventh i wept
because the six were over

the pendulum sway of my inadequate love

from me to she
i am sometimes a blessing
from she to me i am always blessed
tis the painful swing of my love
that you must watch as i abuse a paradise you have grown
whilst i place you recklessly between heaven and hell

desire and design

now that you know i would kiss you
are you scared?
i am
hiding in the shadows of moments we have shared
i lost my soul in the sanctuary of your eyes
excessive in their beauty and control they have
denied me
tied me
disrupted
and defied me

i want to be your primary color
but i am pastel
undefined
and i fear i am not worth you
in the confusion of that line

now that you know i miss you
are you afraid?
i am…
if you fall for me you'll be sorry
if you don't
i will

am i arguing semantics?
better still isn't it romantic
me
wanting to be your primary color

water

carried away
on a wave of surrender
when the last tear fell
into the river you cried
and with every splash you ache
and with every splash you break
like a ripple… across
water

the unforgivingness of porcelain

looked upon the side of your face as you lay next to me in
the night
looked like a porcelain doll in a china shop
wanted to reach out and touch it, caress it
but i couldn't
don't know if it was because i smelled like smoke
or felt like it
so thin and transparent in your life sometimes
feels like i let the moment slip away
like i do so many times
hope you can see within these words
though i didn't touch you
i wanted to

thread-bare

"hanging by a thread"
she said
fuck everything you've bled
take me down the hall where i lay you on the bed
the banging of your head
and the places i am led
when you lay your body bare

hanging by a thread
baby that's your hair
and i'll pull it till it tears
because it's life that is thread-bare

"whatever"
she cried
because i denied
or is it because I deny regardless of how you try
open your legs wide
and let me come inside
when you lay your body bare
hanging by a thread
or is that your fingers in my hair
pulling till we're there
because it's only time that is thread-bare

thread-bare (version 2)

"hanging by a thread"
she said
and i feel everything she's bled
i want to take her down the hall and lay her on the bed
i want to hush the voices inside her head
and the places i am led
when she lays her body bare

hanging by a thread
baby that's my stare
sometimes it's all i wear
when i can't touch to show i care
as your hope unspools thread-bare

"whatever"
she cried
feeling denied
and I cannot deny regardless of how she tries
to let me come inside
sometimes i hide
when she lays her body bare
sometimes i sigh
sometimes i die
"whatever"
she cries

hanging by a thread
keep your fingers in my hair
i need to know you're there
i see you fading from my stare
as the rope unspools thread-bare

hypocrite

because i want to touch you
but you can't touch me when you think of
she
because i want to hold you
but you can't hold what you don't
believe
because i want to kiss you
but you can't kiss what you dismiss
because i want you
but you can't want what you know you miss
why am i the hypocrite?

doves of discontent

it's tragically eminent
some dove of discontent places its heart upon your wings
and starts your decent
lower
lower
lower
until the transformation
and your gentle beak becomes seething fangs
and for the first time, you hit the ground
hard
and you become just another bleeding eye in the land of
wolves
looking to a sky of doves

incidental wind

while walking through a field of confusion
blown into view by an incidental wind that must have read
my mind
was a memory of you
and i thought too long
i thought too long
i should have brushed it away and now you'd be gone
but now i suffer the pain of proximity to youf
ueled by three fires that burn within
of what i
can
can't
and desire to do
maybe i still walk in that field of confusion
swept by a wind
that betrays me again
chaining me with someone i cannot touch
and leaving no solution

st. jude

the sweet belief in hollow faces
only masks their sad disgrace
at believing
there lies something beyond their sadness
even though
that is the seed of their sweet belief

the last conceit of tortured eyes
lies not in what they do not see
but instead what is there before their faces
said and shown with tangible traces
that scars the flesh of sweet beliefs

the soft deceit of bitten lips
is what they bleed but do not speak
instead it's said
but no less sad
the pain that blisters
when they whisper
sweet beliefs

don't go whispering down there

shhh…
words so soft thinner than the air that carries them
away…
before he can hear
and leaving him to fear
shhh…
he imagined what she said…

listen to all the hurting people
listen to all the hurting people
listen to all the hurting people
so silent when they pray
he thought he heard i love you
he thought he heard
shhh…
listen to all the hurting people
don't go whispering down there

pretend i am no one

paper and pen
now and then
before the begin
before you were in
sin after sin
again and again and one without one…
two without, none… before it's begun… before it is done
wind after wind blend after blend
truth that you bend heartache you lend
this is the end again and again
isn't it sunny the sound of her voice
no choice
you fall and all the piano does is keep playing until she's
done with your words…
lento
lento
lento
fingers bleed black white keys
need
and still she brings you in slow
lento
lento
lento

feelings descend
words comprehend
no one will win
it all depends
until you give in
again and again

pretend i am no one (piano pt. 2)

truth believes it knows the way
liars believe in the promises they say l
ight believes in the coming of day
i believe you will never stay
truth believes…
don't deceive

beauty sees what it wants to see
what do you see when you look at me
what do you dream we might be
what will you say when you have to leave
truth believes…
don't deceive
you or me

until you're done with the one you love
pretend i am no one
don't write me songs you know can't be sung
pretend i am no one
everything must go
everyone is starting to know
every song played in this show
everywhere but below
truth believes…
so pretend

Maurice Jovan Billington

23 dolphins

23 dolphins beached themselves today
one two three four five
no one knows why
i hurt you so many times
beautiful creatures
six seven eight
count the times i make mistakes
23 dolphins drowning in air
nine ten
do i care
when i hurt you,
eleven twelve thirteen
fourteen fifteen sixteen
seventeen
it is never what i mean…
did they
mean…
the 23…
to find themselves
on the beach…
or were they looking
eighteen nineteen twenty

twenty-one
for someone that wouldn't hurt them
twenty-two
twenty-three
like me

shallow analysis

i'm sorry.
it took me two hours to write that
that's an hour a word
not too deep
but then there is nothing particularly deep about me
except my love for you
which is why i took two hours to say
i'm sorry

imperfect bliss

This is just a DEMO of feelings
way beyond the first love…THE FIRST ALBUM…
the first kiss
that is
NOT SO SOFT
but IMPERFECTLY bliss
this
LIKE I SAID, is just feelings that sometimes make me feel
dirty and bruised
like a
PUDDLE DIVE , no, dive into a
puddle
but if you look at me
your eyes make me clean though mainly i am seen OUT OF
RANGE
and how does that make you feel
like
NOT A PRETTY GIRL
thinking i haven't chose you
that is not true
your beauty DIALATEs
wider as the time passes and i find myself
LIVING IN CLIPs of moments gone but cherished
like a child's LITTLE PLASTIC CASTLE
if i am down by one without you

i am UP UP UP UP UP UP within you
i am TO THE TEETH i am REVELLING…
RECKONING…i am
not SO MUCH SHOUTING but SO MUCH
LAUGHTER because i have
EVOLVED
and my
EDUCATED GUESS would be to KNUCKLE DOWN in
this
imperfect bliss

blood flowers

he asked, "can i trust you when i'm gone?"
she replied, "if you have to ask, it's wrong."
he said, "only flowers don't need
and anything that does will eventually bleed."
she said, nothing…
but she gave him a kiss and when he wiped his lips he swore there was blood.

the space of hearts

am i losing her in the space of hearts
where little girls discard plastic boys
packing them away like a baby's toys
on a shelf of forgotten disdain
to remember a time
where memories serve
easing another lover's pain

i said pick a card any card
and so she chose the space of hearts
the joker's wild
but that's his style
and now he's playing solitaire

am i losing her in the space of hearts
where girls dismiss their futile dreamers
where one by one romantic schemers
slowly die worlds apart

i said pick a card

in light of this derailment

all i can say as you walk out that door
is why do i love what i don't want anymore
do i need what i love
do i love what i need
is movement the same at two different speeds
do i give what i take
do i take what i gave
if it all came from you
and i never questioned its truth
does that make me your slave
then was my love used as chains
if so give me the key before you catch your next train

enter the mythic
(the chaos of her smile pt. 1)

saw a wild-eyed boy from freecloud
no one gets out alive
beyond the place where the heartbreakers lay
i rode the calm horse of your laughter
they look at me
sad eyes wonder why
nothing i could do
searching for you
and them
they look for the way out
the way they got in
through the chaos of your smile

absolute beguiling
(the chaos of her smile pt. 2)

there are no absolutes
and nothing that beguiles
save the mythic truth
that when i see you smiling
it's absolute divineness
absolute beguiling

the mythic
(the chaos of her smile pt. 3)

i rode the calm horse of your laughter thru
past the chaos of your smile
just to get to you
and i saw your naked flesh
i touched your porcelain skin
i brushed across your breasts
i felt myself within

easel
(a series of poems as art)

—gouache—
(easel pt. 1)

egg white paste
dripping from your hands
melting tears of clay
painting me missing you

-impressionism-
(easel pt. 2)

his desire for her
was the powder that covered her hands
after she had been drawing
with chalk
if he could
he would
cover her in it
and make her an impression of his love

-self portrait-
(easel pt. 3)

?
can i draw that
is that how you see me
whisper the answer in my ear
I still won't be able to draw it
but at least you will be close
does that tell you about myself
?

-sketch-
(easel pt. 4)

he fell in love so fast
she didn't even have time to draw a sketch
he lost his heart
before she could get pencil in hand

-self portrait pt. 2-
(easel pt. 5)

if i were to draw myself
taking my image from the reflection in your eyes
when you're looking at me
in the darkness of who we are
where we are
what we are doing
i would pencil myself entirely in
black
then take the eraser and erase a line
one line
that is the emptiness i feel
after you have closed your eyes
and i am no longer there

-watercolors-
(easel pt. 6)

it's so dark where i live
what is that color i see
is that you wanting me
is that you wanting me
is that you
wanting
me
thirsty
i need water
and to know what
color
i see

-brushstroke-
(easel pt. 7)

i wish that i drew words
the way that you draw breath
i'd keep repeating like a painter with only one color

      stay

      stay

      stay

—gouache pt. 2—
(easel pt. 8)

gouache
are you as pretty
as that word sounds
and do my lips burn
when i say it
like when we kiss
gouache

−surrealism−
(easel pt. 9)

his desire
draw myself
dripping
egg white
she didn't even have
time…
water
dripping
is that… powder
where we are
painting me pretty
as that sounds
cover her in it
reflection
so dark
so fast
sketches of
melting tears
erase
missing you
and do my lips burn…
?

broken nail

i was staring at your broken nail
wondering if that was how your heart was broken
and will it grow back
together
did your heart break like your nail
was it fast
was it painful
did i rip it with one careless act

or

did i slowly chip away pieces scattered about 2 years i was
supposed to make you happy
i don't know how your nail broke
but i know how your heart did
i didn't mean it
you're not psychotic
i am
for saying that when i meant to say i love you
and it is OK to cry
because it hurts when your nail is broken
i should know that but i'm stupid
i didn't even buy you a present yesterday
valentines day

is that why you woke up this morning smelling like tears
or is it because you broke your nail
or is it because i broke your heart
or is it because you're afraid only one will grow back

ether or

blood on the floor
mine or yours
doesn't matter anymore
ether or
you walk out that door

i don't love you anymore

all the things she said

Early morning
Birthdays, Holidays
I never seem to get any closer
Love you
Only because you're away
I've been feeling it since May.
Tell her too
We're all a wreck
And one big lie
Pick a point and go.
They say you can't ask this of me
Your sad face
Ever so persuasive
This is how you want to live.
I see a brave new world
But in an instant
Your interest shifts and
My stream of consciousness breaks

I can only trust your intentions are benevolent.

on my honor i pledge to ache

He said
There's nowhere to go but down
There's not enough here for you
But you won't learn
And you won't be happy
And without a thought
He smirked and turned his back
Learn or leave
And don't expect a thing
He scorned
You won't feel it til we hit the ground
Be sure to hold my hand
And tell me how beautiful I am
On the way down
I act differently
But I promise I still feel the same
You're special
But the saga has an end
You're sophomoric maturity
Makes us both weary
Now brace for impact

The wreckage will leave me copasetic
I'll be fine baby
He turns his back on devastation

Tonight he won't have to say the words she wanted.

wonky belly

she gives me a wonky belly
5 hours away
pick up a potato chip and burn your mouth
i can't believe i like this
oh man
here comes the converse
here comes the dance
cowboys
black boys
all a a part of her barroom toys
here come the muse-ings
she don't wear shoe strings
5 hours away
was i sleeping when my hand slipped away
from yours
she keeps her clothes scattered on the floor
maybe that's why we didn't crash
kittens are soft
hello
not ready to say goodbye
she still makes my belly wonky

hurts

i do love you, i just miss you.
a friend wrote me and it made me miss you more
your buddies get to play with you and it made me miss you more
we talked about how we will meet and it made me miss you more
i woke up and it made me miss you more
i can't miss you anymore and i'm still missing you more
and it hurts

black raspberry chip

if I were asked how would I like her
in a bowl or a cup
i'd say, 'All over my face!'
like Black Raspberry Chip
Ice cream…

wednesday before

she said, "It's Tuesday where i am."
my life was 7 hours behind her
but what she didn't realize
was at the rate my heart began beating when i heard her
voice
it propelled me into Wednesday
where i already waited with a kiss

a locked door from the floor in the sky

pull down your pants
where heaven is contained
do not worry
whose flying the plane
it won't go down
i will
and remain
spread your legs
my god
i think i just came…

shhh
your moans will alert the sky
to our violation

that isn't knocking
it's my heart dropping to the floor
more
more
more
your feet against the door
give me more
my dirty whore
give me more
and if we should plummet to the ocean floor
the words i whispered in your ear
before the crash
before the splash
were i love you.

untitled 11

Her hand
within
the forgiveness of a thousand angels
portends
nothing in my past matters anymore

forever is a heart with 3 chambers

i like you a lot
i love you even more
i want to fuck you more than both right now
print this on your tongue

V

one can only imagine Cupid's arrow is envious
that you're able to do its job
without benefit
of a
bow

hairline fractured

hair...
soft to touch
where there shouldn't be
there...
between her sighs
where i cannot flee

brush against my face
and leave me in this place

unfinished

days
lack
i'm back
who yells the first attack
and is it written in the lines running down my back
from you

it's in the blood
anything i am guilty of
and i can't sit there and watch you bleed
waiting for the things you say you need
from me

unfinished II

truth
soothe
either way
win or lose
and why when you cry are your eyes
only blue

woke up
could not sleep
no sign of you
no sign of me
just this paper – i started to write
before a flight i had to make
better i don't know why i stopped
why you stopped
why we stopped
but here it is unfinished
a child's half smile
your clothes in a pile
it won't go away in awhile
my head won't
let it

it's in the blood

hippo-promises

she is so cute
like the space between a hippo's tooth
she has legs that go to her
cheekbones
you need a ladder to kiss her
i am glad i am tall
and that she promised to paint a hippo for me
so i can give her a big hippo kiss
with lots of tongue
'cause hippos have big tongues

apple

and like this
taste
as with every
indiscretion
blood
but i am willing to bathe
in the red
until i am covered
in the entirety
of every regret
we ran into
willingly

candles and other things that burn without the benefit of control

ache
is a candle
aware of its length
but not its
wick
leaving it no choice
but to burn
and
wonder
if the very thing that makes it what it is
will extinguish
before it is ready
to stop loving you

cicatrix

you wash over me
like drops of
water
unsure
if they should
remain
and be absorbed
into my skin
it is that uncertainty
that makes
the water burn
leaving a scar
that only more water
will soothe

the blue space beside you

it is everything
it is
nothing
it is whatever you bring
surrounds like
blue

count the rings
two
you see
blue again
in everything

tattoo
you
tattoos too
tattoo everything
blue

it is everything
it is…
nothing

husssh

her finger tried to keep secret
everything her face freely revealed
even her closed eyes
laughed
at the futility
of her hand's
gesture

arachnophobia and other things that don't require the dark but work better without light

she has a tattoo of a spider on her arm
doesn't she know boys are afraid of spiders
maybe she doesn't care
maybe that's why it's there
she's posing silly with her head against her head
like she's trying to keep a headache in
who does that?
girls with spiders on their arm
her smile is almost completely lit
perhaps that's what her hand is doing
attempting to block the light
but who would do that?
besides girls with spiders on their arm
and even with her eyes half closed
she still tries to obscure them with her hair
which lays across them like the strands of a web
maybe that's why there's a tattoo of a spider on her arm
because it's waiting to see who the light attracts
or maybe it's just there
like the part of her smile
hidden in the dark

searchers have found hardly any human remains at all

>   in a sky
>   as wide
>   how can
>   we collide
>   leaving nothing
>   but the impact

the last line of hell and grace

a men

Poems From A Portion

(the following are poems from my novel A Portion Of The Eternal)

the envy of angels

in the highest of places they watch
some almost fall with their anger
this is why they are needed
this is why they are here
but in your arms their existence is unnecessary
and angels get caught as they stare

my father

he writes so beautifully
but he lives in its ruins
day to day everything he gives to explain
only takes away leaving nothing
he could write a smile
it will return to him as rain
my father writes so beautifully
but I've never heard him laugh

eternal nothing

nothing is eternal
not the daylight.
nor the night.
nothing last forever except the pain
knowing I will never see you again

nothing is eternal
how can it be
when we are not
because we are
nothing

nothing is eternal
not even nothing
even though nothing
remains the same after it is gone

some...where

somewhere a bell is ringing
somewhere a bride has died
somewhere a dove escapes
somewhere a groomsman lied
somewhere there is cake that shall never melt
somewhere there is a day that will never be felt

the overflow

water spills from your eyes
but tears do not wash away pain
they only empty the soul to store more hurt
rain
i will be your pool
empty into me
until I overflow
then empty again

carrion of his absence

i am the carrion of his absence
i am this that remains
empty
do not call my name
lest the birds know where to feast

pools of you

the sky is a pool of blue
clouds crash like waves
i am told
when you look up
and rain cascades
to dive into you

breakfast is dying

what lies beneath a Sunday sky?
the weeping of a child, his lullaby?
wake mother, breakfast is dying on the table

the father opens his eyes.
an impression of where his love once laid remains.
feathers will one day suffocate him

if you drink the coffee too fast
mother
your lips will burn

if you look at the sun too long
daughter
your eyes will melt

take thy father's hand
there are gestures grand
this day holds the promise of

walk outside into the closing sky
birds fly
one day their feathers will suffocate them
and they will fall
at your feet

It's alright.
they were only supposed to be in the sky
until you saw them

sometimes dark

sometimes
it is only when I look
into the darkness
that I am able to see myself.
and I am almost always smiling.
and I am almost never alone.
though I am the only one I can see.
warm like a lullaby.
resigned like a sigh
will you ever let me go?
will you ever let me die

trumpets

your eyes compel like the trumpet of angels.
is that why I feel as if I've died?
as if my soul were being emptied of everything I was and everything I could be because now it has changed.
did you steal my eternity before you blinked?
and when I look into your eyes again, is that why I see me inside?
how cruel your gaze
how gentle your smile
how is it possible
they both beguile

there is no death but love

there is no death in me but love
the love of things
holding hands
your eyes
sodomizing dragonflies
with you.
there is no death in me but love
no desert promises
no beauty of ruins
but there is always your smile when Kinski is on screen.
there is no death in me but love
and this is how I know the wind is a mistaken name
and that all monsters dark are necessary
and that you wouldn't want to make the same mistake twice
for every gesture frail
for every somewhere a bell is ringing
lies the threat of the dissipating dusk
and me becoming the carrion of his absence
the abandoned and the reborn.
there is no death in me but love
this is how I know the beach is no place for lovers
this is how I know there is a fountain that burns
and that if I ask do animals have souls they sell
the response will bounce off the echo of rocks.
there is no death in me but love

so onto whom does the blood from your fingers fall
and if the perscussionist pauses for a piece of candy
will he gain riches
or will the rabbit the lion and the wind
carry his beat and whisper whores
to those that dive into pools of you?
there is no death in me but love
this is how I know there are no accidental gestures
no happy fracture
no resurrection
but my heart will still beat
with the momentum of sons
greater than a feigning corpse
whose death becomes revenge by mourning
graced with strawberry intentions.
there is no death in me but love
and if his eye was the pen of his greatest work
that work reaps more havoc than the desecration of thunder
and if it is a choice between bourbon and caramel
if it is the distinction between Nabakov the girl on the wall
and the one in the bed
I will whisper cicada
but I will not name you for fear you will never leave
nor will I admire the briefness of the beauty of snow
but I will look into your eyes

I will feel the rev of a carousel
I will fight the imposing decay
I will close every door to partial rooms
to get you to stay
and close these breaches of faith
reminding me with your silly way
that only every third word counts.
There is no death in me but love
this is how I know silhouettes are not the ghosts you run
from but the ghosts you become
and if one asks, do you want to fuck
you have begun the long ascent up the downward
and something so pretty as the color magenta
will not stop the reverse of a carousel
that is taking away your dreams
of things like Deschanel
and horses pulling promises underwater.
there is no death in me but love
thus none of my tears are untitled
and I know if I am to hold onto you I must kiss the
resurrected curse the dead and be careful not to confuse the
two
speaking of two
we are sometimes two awkward hippos

but I love you so much there is no door I will not walk
through to get back to you not even death
and I would read algebra and Ecclesiastes
and I would protect every kiss before Judas
to keep our souls intertwined
and dancing like flickers

father

you are my father
i am the portion of you you chose to release
but I am the portion that will always return
for I am the portion of you, eternal

Excerpts From The Book I Never Wrote

(the following are isolated paragraphs from the book Narcissistic Racist Pricks And Other People To Envy)

the consequence of babes

I innocently called her, 'babe.' She hated it when I called her babe. I hated it even more that she wasn't one. But I was trying this new thing where I used adjectives alphabetically and yesterday was A. I couldn't wait until I saw her tomorrow. If every man that ever wanted a woman to shut up were homicidal the Earth would eventually have a population of 2. And they would probably be lesbians. Even then, at some point, one of them would want the other one to shut the fuck up. I think that's what happened to the dinosaurs.

Jameson

She said, 'Jameson was the best whiskey ever.' She was a girl so I let her finish the sentence without correcting her. I wanted to spit out the Jack Daniels I had just consumed but I couldn't because it was Jack Daniels. So I waited for the guy sitting next to me to take a sip of his Canadian Club then punched him in the throat. There's your spit take. I looked over at the girl. I wanted to put my hand up her skirt but she took another drink of Jameson and I decided to stick my tongue in my glass of Jack instead. She could tell she blew it. I heard her whisper as I turned to the redhead that had the sense not to speak, "Fuck the Irish."

Huh

She turned around with great anticipation. Like a stripper expecting a hamburger made of meth to appear once she rounded the pole. I knew she was trouble from the moment she started talking. I hated that in some women. The ability to talk. 'I'm married,' I told her. 'I even have a ring to prove it. Unfortunately some hooker in Fresno stole it off the hotel nightstand so you'll have to take my word for it.' The hookers in Fresno were all thieves... But they knew how to take a punch. She asked me if I was strong enough to be her man. I said, "Huh?" Huh to women was like headlights to a deer. I just stood there waiting for a car to hit her.

Dexy

Her name was Eileen, and no, no one had come on her, but there was a donkey in Boise waiting to give her a punch. It was clear I was going to have to endure her voice until I was willing to suck on the business end of a 45. Even then I'm sure I'd still be able to hear her bitching about there not being enough different kinds of cheese at the wake. I'm positive one of her relatives knew Van Gogh. Undoubtedly he was about to cut his 'other' ear off when mercifully syphilis took him first. She said I should expand my views on women. I told her the only view of women I liked was from behind. And it almost always expanded me. She didn't find that funny, so I bought her a free ticket to Boise. Then I called the donkey and told him to put his mouthpiece in.

Poker Hands

She was cute but she knew it which made her more annoying than an ugly girl that didn't realize she was ugly. I didn't need cute. I was cute. That didn't mean I wanted to fuck myself. Cute was a poker hand and there were plenty of women holding a pair so why sit at the table with attitude. I looked around for something more interesting. Like a wall. I saw a special kid across the room about to eat a plate of hot wings without any ranch dressing on the side. Poor bastard didn't know what he was in for. She told me she was a single mother. I told her single mothers were like movies with too many previews. She slapped me. Like the saying goes, 'If you can't stand the heat, don't be born a woman, because sooner or later you're needed in the kitchen.' I picked up her ranch dressing and walked over to my special friend for a lesson in eating hot wings and some adult conversation.

Juries Jokes Jokes Jury

OJ Simpson, Casey Anthony and George Zimmerman walk into a bar. OJ asks Casey if she wants money for the babysitter. Casey says she's didn't need one. Zimmerman asks Anthony if she saw the suspicious looking black kid eyeing their car. Casey says that was the valet. George goes, oops. Both ask OJ how much they will need to tip the waiter after the meal. OJ says, don't worry I'll take care of him. God is sitting at the bar, he shakes his head, downs his shot and asks the bartender how can juries be so fu*king dumb.

about the author

Maurice Jovan Billington is both an author and an award winning screenwriter. His debut novel, *A Portion of the Eternal*, is available in bookstores and on Amazon. He is also the writer/director of the independent short film "The Horizon Bleeds and Sucks Its Thumb."

Contact him at Mauricejovan@aol.com.

by this author:

Innocence stolen. Love denied. Liv finds herself torn, haunted by memories of her dead boyfriend, tormented by those who may have killed him, and drawn to a mysterious new student who brings with him not only redemption and revenge, but the chance for her to live again.

Read more at APortionofTheEternal.com.

Made in the USA
Middletown, DE
06 October 2020